Movement Stories

8 STORIES IN ONE!

Busy Little Bugs

Blast Off!

Crash, Bang, Build!

The Monster Conga Line

Swish, Splash Swim!

My First Rugby Game

Rain Bubble Pop!

Nick Clement

A book by Confident Healthy Active Me CIC
Where Kinesthetic Literacy Comes to Life

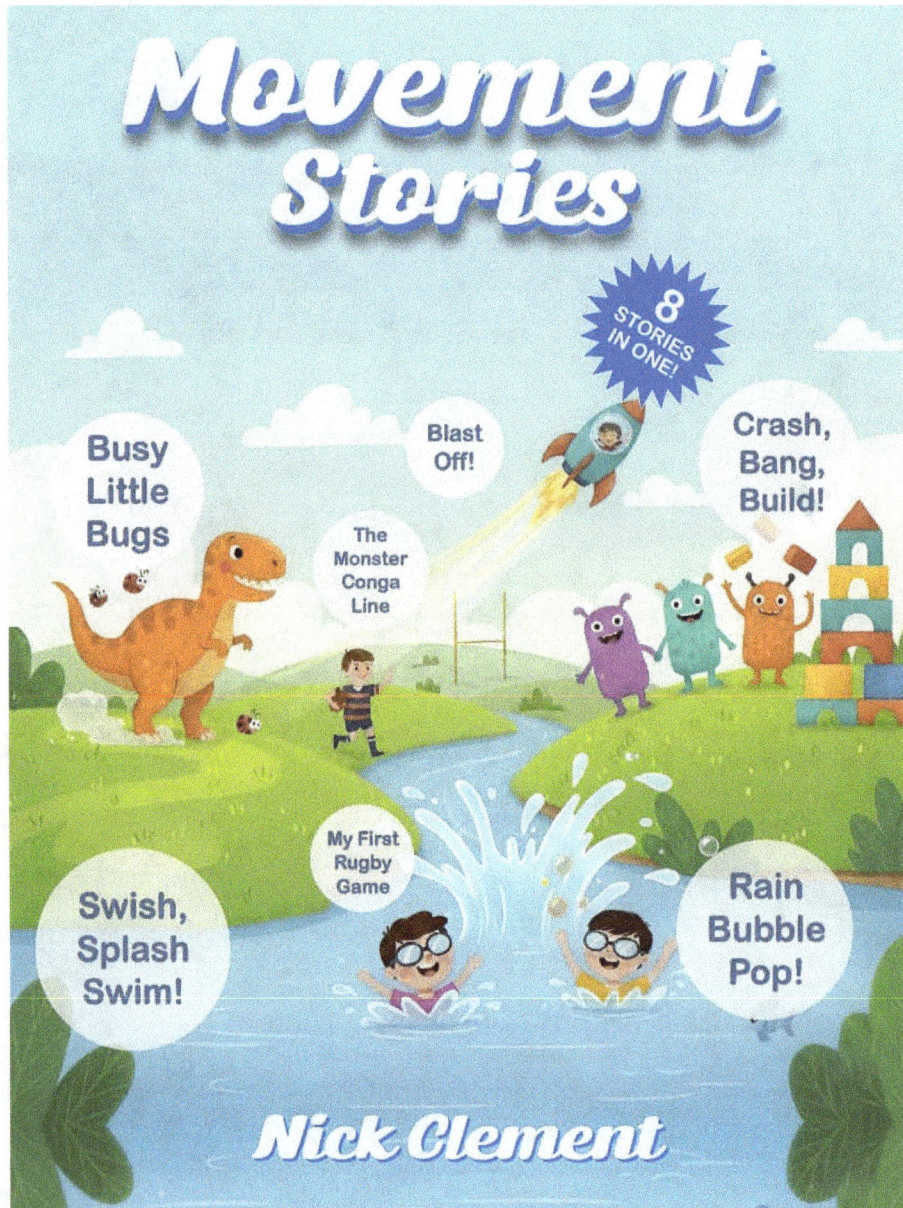

Movement Stories

8 STORIES IN ONE!

Busy Little Bugs

Blast Off!

Crash, Bang, Build!

The Monster Conga Line

My First Rugby Game

Swish, Splash Swim!

Rain Bubble Pop!

Nick Clement

An interactive movement story to get little bodies moving and big imaginations flying!

Table of Contents

About Confident Healthy Active Me CIC

Confident Healthy Active Me (CHAM) is a Wales-based community interest company helping children grow in confidence, health and happiness through movement, creativity and play. We believe that confidence starts with health and action — and that every child deserves the chance to move, explore and feel proud of who they are.

What We Do

- Movement-Based Learning: Fun, inclusive sessions for schools, nurseries and families.
- Creative Storytelling: Action-packed movement stories that make learning active and joyful.
- Teacher & Parent Resources: Simple tools to bring wellbeing and confidence into daily life.
- Community Collaboration: Working with schools, councils and charities to reach every child.

www.confidentactive.com

How to Use This Book

This is a movement-based story. Each page includes an action for children to copy. Read the story aloud and guide the movements as you go.

1. Before You Start

- Make a little space so children can move safely.
- Invite them to stand, stretch and get ready to join in.

2. How to Read and Move

- Read each line clearly, with rhythm and expression.
- Pause on the action line and show the movement yourself or model slowly.
- Encourage children to copy the action in their own way — big, small, fast, slow.

3. Keeping Children Engaged

- Use your voice to match the story (quiet for sneaking, loud for jumping, etc.)
- Let children choose how big or small their movements are.
- Celebrate effort, not correctness — the aim is fun, movement and imagination.

Tips for Parents, Carers & Teachers

Children don't need to perform the actions perfectly — participation is the goal. If a child prefers seated movement, adapt the actions so they can still join in. You can turn the story into a whole session: warm-up → story → cool down.

Repeat the same story on different days — movements become smoother with practice. Ask at the end: "Which movement did you like best?" or "Can you invent a new action for the story?"

Why Movement Matters

Movement is one of the most powerful tools for children's learning and development. Every jump, stretch and spin helps build the foundations for confidence, coordination and emotional wellbeing.

Brain Development When children move, both sides of the brain are engaged. Activities that cross the body's midline, involve balance or require coordination strengthen neural pathways that support attention, memory and problem-solving. Regular movement helps to "wire" the brain for learning, supporting language, reading and concentration.

Gross and Fine Motor Skills Large, whole-body actions such as running, climbing and balancing develop gross motor skills that build strength, posture and control. Smaller, more precise actions such as clapping, grasping and manipulating objects refine fine motor skills, preparing children for writing and self-care tasks.

Emotional and Physical Wellbeing Active play releases energy, improves mood and reduces stress. Physical movement supports the release of endorphins and helps children regulate emotions, build confidence and develop resilience.

Social Connection Moving together encourages communication, teamwork and empathy. Shared physical play creates belonging and trust, which are essential for healthy relationships and confident learning.

At Confident Healthy Active Me CIC, we believe that movement, creativity and play form the heart of a healthy childhood — because confidence starts with health and action.

CRASH, BANG, BUILD!

Nick Clement

In partnership with Confident Healthy Active Me CIC

Crash goes the hammer, bang goes the wall,
Stamp your feet, we're strong and tall!
(Stamp feet loudly and proudly)

Bang with your hands, clap them tight, Let's build
a tower, big and bright!
*(Clap hands loudly, then slowly stretch arms
upwards)*

Beep, beep, back it up slow, Tiptoe backwards,
nice and low.
(Tiptoe backwards carefully, slow and steady)

Push the dirt, dig the ground, Big strong arms go
round and round!
(Circle arms like scooping dirt)

Crash down bricks, one, two, three, Jump and shout "Build with me!"
(Jump up and shout happily)

Bang on your knees, tap your toes, The building's higher — up it goes!
(Kneel and tap toes or clap knees and feet)

Now the machines are slowing down, Stretch up high, then touch the ground.
(Big stretch up, slow bend to floor)

Lay down flat, the work is done, Crash, bang, build — that was fun!
(Lie flat on back, gentle breathing to calm)

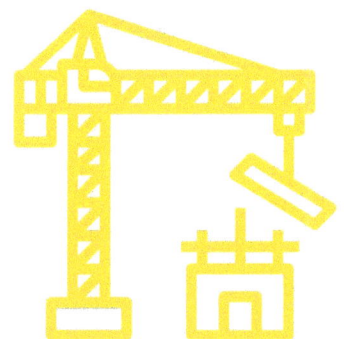

Rain Bubble Pop

By Confident Healthy Active Me CIC

Bubbles bounce and bubbles fly — Let's JUMP up high and reach the sky!
(Children jump and pop the bubbles)

Bubbles zoom and spin so fast, Spin your body — not too fast!
(Children spin slowly)

They float and shimmer in the sun, Pop them gently — just with one!
(Children pop bubbles with one finger)

Clap your hands to make a sound, Bubbles swirling all around!
(Clapping to rhythm)

Now lay down and close your eyes, Feel the bubbles float and rise...
(Children lie down and imagine bubbles popping on their body)

Bubbles drift near toes and knees, Kick them gently with your feet!
(Kicking bubbles away with feet while seated or reclined)

Shhhh... the wind is soft and slow, Now sway your arms and let it go.

(Gentle swaying)

Lay down gently on the floor, The bubbles come... there's even more!

(Lying flat)

Tiny toes up in the air — Kick the bubbles everywhere!

(Feet up, kicking softly while lying down)

And now we rest, our bubbles done, What a day of bubble fun.

(Deep breath, quiet time)

Busy Little Bugs

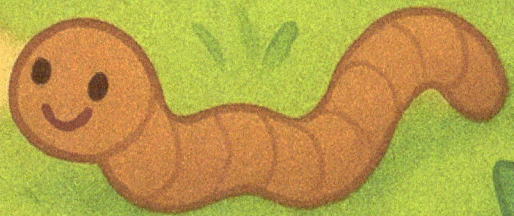

Bugs

By Nick Clement

Busy Little Bugs

Garden Clean up

It's a bright, sunny morning in the garden, The flowers are blooming, and the leaves are swirling around! The bugs are busy getting ready for a big garden cleanup— Will you help them? Let's get moving and make the garden shine!

First, we have the ants! The ants are marching, working hard, Carrying food and cleaning the yard! Let's move like ants, all in a line, Crawl on the floor, one by one, so fine!

(Crawl on the floor, moving like ants, busy and focused.)

The butterflies are fluttering in the air, They're helping the flowers, flying here and there. Now we'll be butterflies, flying so free, Flap your arms gently, as light as can be!

(Flutter your arms like butterfly wings, soaring gracefully.)

Next, we have the busy worms below, They're digging the soil to make it all glow! Let's wiggle like worms, wriggling so deep, Dig through the dirt where the flowers sleep!
(Wiggle your body side to side, as if digging deep into the ground.)

The ladybugs are coming to the rescue, They help tidy up, and they know what to do! Let's be ladybugs, hopping along, Move like a ladybug, hopping strong!
(Hop lightly, just like ladybugs hopping from leaf to leaf.)

Uh-oh! The leaves have fallen from the trees, They're all over the ground, blowing in the breeze! Let's help by sweeping them all away, Use your hands to sweep the leaves, let's tidy today!
(Pretend to sweep the ground with your hands, gathering up the leaves.)

Look at that, the garden's all clean, The flowers are bright, and the bugs are serene. The ants march back to their little home, The butterflies flutter back to their dome. But now it's time to take a break, The work is done —let's rest for goodness' sake!

The sun sets low, and the sky turns blue, The bugs have worked hard, and so have you!
(Relax and take a deep breath together.)

The
Monster
Conga Line
A Movement Story

By Nick Clement

THE MONSTER CONGA LINE

It's a fun day in Monsterland, And all the monsters are taking a stand. The conga line starts with a wiggle and a spin, So join in, and let the dancing begin!
First, we wiggle our hips, side to side, Like a monster who's having a wild ride!

(Wiggle your hips from side to side, like you're shimmying along.)

Then comes the stomp, stomp, stomp, so loud,
The monsters stomp their feet, feeling proud!
Let's stomp our feet, stomp with all might,
Stomp so hard, we make the ground shake right!

(Stomp feet in place, like you're a big, strong monster.)

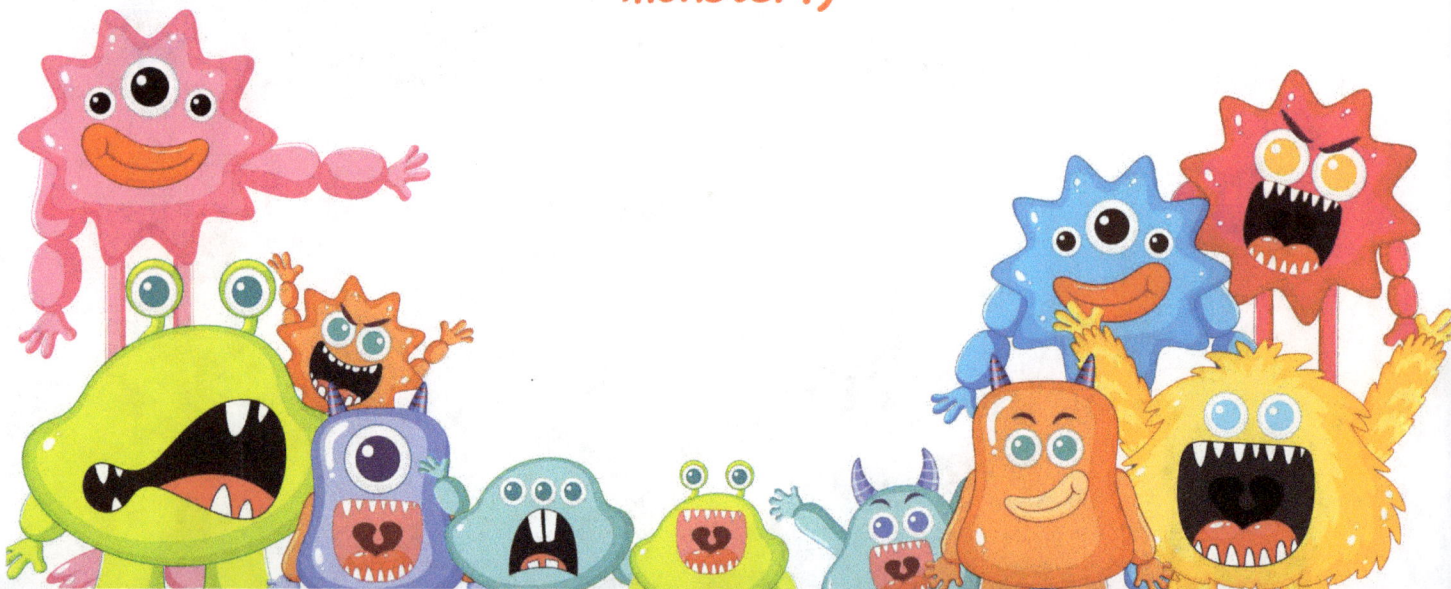

Next, here comes the 20-legged monster, Kick, kick, kick
with legs getting bolder!

Balance on one foot, then kick your leg out, Like a
20-legged monster, give a big shout!
*(Balance on one foot, then kick one leg out and
switch to the other.)*

The conga line keeps growing long,
With each new monster singing their song!

Now, let's spin, spin, spin around,
Let's go round and round and make a funny sound!

Spin like a whirlwind, round and round, Then stop
real quick, with your feet on the ground!
(Spin around in a circle, and stop in place.)

Time to balance, let's make it fun,

Can you balance without falling, everyone?

Lift one leg, stretch your arms out wide, Stay
steady as a monster – no wobble or slide!
*(Balance on one leg, arms out for balance—hold it
steady!)*

Uh-oh! The monsters are getting tired, But wait, the
fun's not over, it's time to get wired!

Now slide to the left, slide to the right, Slide like a
monster, with all your might!
*(Slide to one side, then the other, with big, fun
steps.)*

Let's all jump in the conga line, Jumping up and down,
feeling fine!

Jump up high, then jump down low, Bounce like a monster,
ready to go!
*(Jump up high, then crouch down low, bouncing in
rhythm.)*

The conga line is long and wide, The monsters keep dancing, side by side.

Now let's all freeze – stay still as can be, The monsters freeze too, just like you and me!

Let's finish the dance with a big monster spin, Then end with a roar – let the fun begin!

(Spin around one more time, then end with a big monster roar!)

We did it! The conga line is complete, The monsters danced to the beat!

From spinning, jumping, and kicking our legs, To wiggling, sliding, and shaking our heads.

DON'T WAKE
THE T-REX!

By Nick Clement

Don't Wake the T-Rex

Deep in the jungle, the sun's rising high, The birds chirp and the monkeys swing by. We're off on a mission, a secret quest, But first, we must tiptoe – the T-Rex needs rest!

(Tiptoe low, tiptoe slow... shhh, quiet steps...)

He's snoring so loud, the trees start to shake! He twitches his toes and gives a big wake! We creep through the vines, don't make a sound, As quiet as a mouse, we move all around! Climb over a log, stretch up to the sky, Now duck under branches, don't be shy.
Now freeze like a statue, no wiggles at all... SHHHH! Was that a rumble or a leaf's soft fall?

(Pretend to climb and duck)

(Big reach, crouch low, then FREEZE!)

Then... UH-OH! A SNAP! A CRACK! A THUMP! The T-Rex wakes with a ROAR and a jump! "WHO DARES DISTURB MY DINO DREAM?" He roars so loud, the parrots scream!

(Jump up! Stomp your feet! Give a BIG RAAAAWR!)

"RUN!" we shout – it's time to dash, Through the mud, we slip and splash! Hop on the rocks, then crawl down low, Quick through the leaves – go, go, go!

(Run in place, hop side to side, crawl low...)

We jump through the ferns, then hide in a tree.

T-Rex stomps past... but doesn't see me! He sniffs and

snorts, "Where did they go?" Then shrugs his big

shoulders, nice and slow.

(Climb up high, then crouch and peek...)

"I guess I'll go back to my nap," he said, Then flopped on his tummy and rested his head.
We tiptoed back, no longer afraid, That T-Rex chase sure made our day!
(Tiptoe again, then wiggle with joy!)

Let's do our dino dance – we earned it, you bet! The best kind of fun is the fun with a sweat! Stomp, wiggle, jump, and ROAR, Then curl up small and move no more.
(Dino dance party! Then curl up like you're going to sleep...)

Swish, Splash, Swim!

By Nick Clement

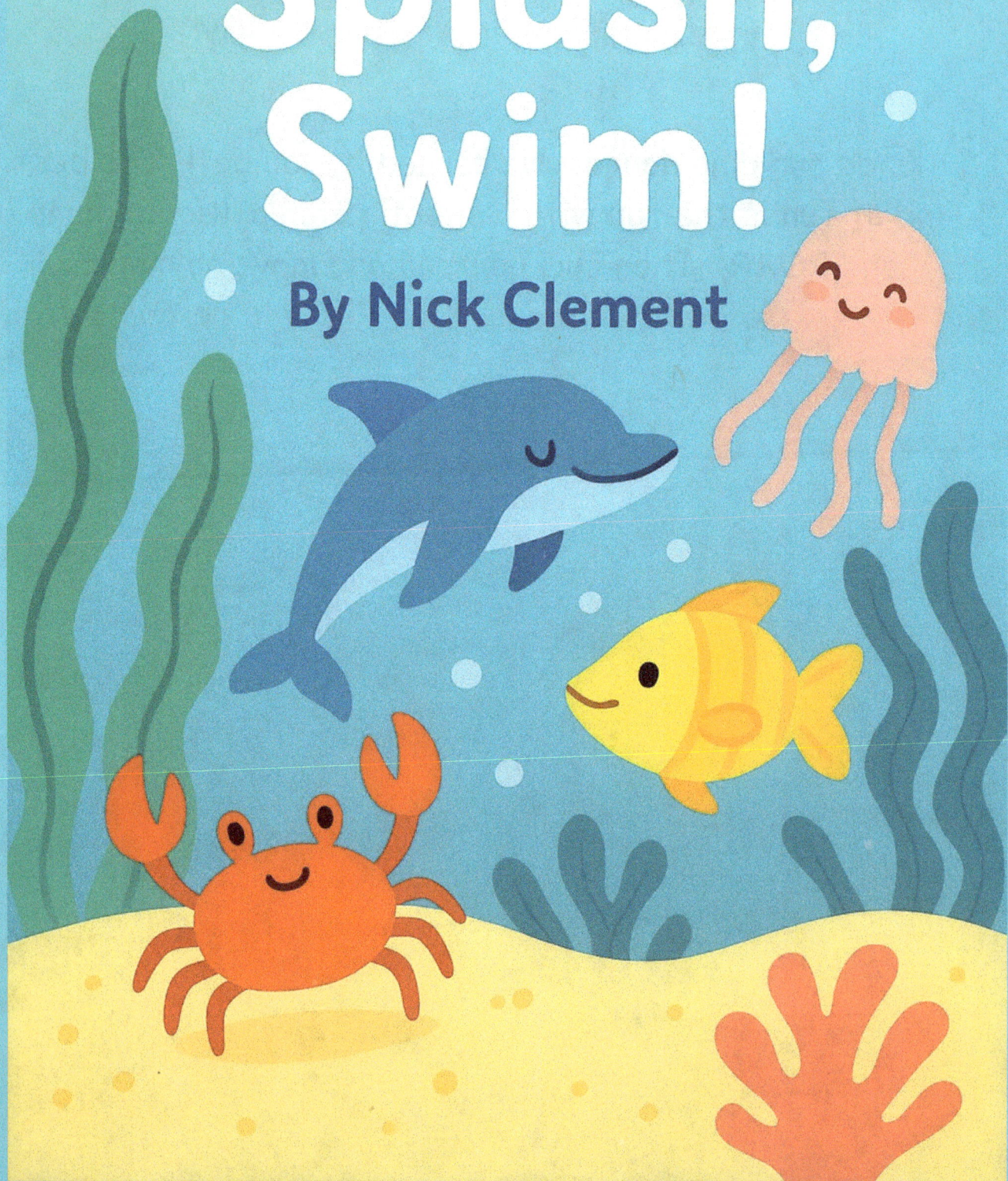

Swish, Splash, Swim!

Splash in the rock pools, splash in the sun, Paddle your feet — the swim has begun!

(Paddle feet, splashing on the spot)

Wiggle your fingers, reach up high, Wave to the seagulls flying by.

(Wiggle fingers up to the sky)

Creep like a crab across the sand, Sideways shuffle, hand to hand!

(Sideways walking, crab claws with hands)

Balance on one foot, wobble and sway, The waves are rocking you today!

(Balance on one foot, gentle swaying)

Dive under seaweed, bend down low, Swish your arms and off you go!
(Bend and swish arms like seaweed moving)

Swim like a fish, glide left and right,
Swoosh your body, light and bright!
(Sway body side to side like a swimming fish)

Snap like a shrimp and bounce on your toes,
Tiny jumps as the sea breeze blows!
(Tiny jumps up and down lightly)

Float like a jellyfish, soft and slow,
Arms drifting gently to and fro.
(Arms float and sway loosely)

Now stretch out wide, a starfish at rest, Lie down flat — you've done your best!
(Lie flat on the floor, arms and legs stretched out)

Close your eyes, the sea sings near, Swish, splash, swim — we're safe right here.
(Gentle breathing and resting time)

Blast Off!

By Nick Clement

Blast Off

Put on your boots, zip up tight — Our rocket's flying off tonight!
(Pretendto put on space boots and zip up your suit)

Tuck in your gloves and helmet too, We've got a space trip just for you!
(Pathands, tap head — pretend to fasten gear)

Check the buttons, spin around, Let's get ready — countdown sound!
(Tap pretend buttons, then spin)

Press the lever, beep-beep-beep, Rocket ready, on your feet!
(Make beep sounds, stand tall)

Crouch down low and hold in tight... The rocket's ready for its flight!

(Crouch low like you're loading into the rocket)

Engines rumble, feel the floor, We're ready now — let's soar and roar!

(Tap floor, sway side to side like rumbling)

5... 4... 3... 2... 1 —

BLAST OFF now, jump to the sun!

(Jump up high with arms zooming forward)

Arms out wide, now rocket fly! Let's zoom and zigzag through the sky.

(Arms out, zigzag running in place)

Zooming fast through the air, Fly your arms — we're almost there!

(Arms forward, running or zooming in place)

Dodge a comet, duck down low, Keep on flying — go, go, go!

(Duck and rise, repeat with rhythm)

Look around, the stars are bright, Wave hello — it's a starry night!

(Wave and spin gently on the spot)

Twinkle toes and tiptoe wide, Across the moon with careful stride.

(Tiptoe walk with sparkle fingers)

Drift back down, our trip is done, We've danced with stars and touched the sun. Close your eyes, the sky turns deep

Time to land and fall asleep.

(Lay down slowly on the floor)

This Book Has Been Kindly Sponsored by Wales Rugby League

- Transforming lives through rugby league.

- We want every child to have the opportunity to play rugby league, because we know that active children are happier and healthier.

- Our partnership with CHAM CIC and your school is giving children that chance.

- Find out more and read our strategy at www.wrl.wales

WALES RUGBY LEAGUE,
The Lextan Gnoll,
Gnoll Park Road,
Neath
SA11 3BT.

My First Rugby Game

Let's start with a warm-up, and stretch real high, Stretch the balloon up to the sky!

(Reach the balloon overhead, stretching up high with both hands.)

Now, let's bend down low and touch our toes, Keep the balloon close, as it goes where it goes!

(Bend down and gently touch your toes, keeping the balloon close to the body.)

It's time for a twist! Let's twist left and right, Twist with the balloon, and feel the light!

(Twist your body to the left and right while holding the balloon.)

Now, we're ready to play! Let's pass the balloon and start our day!

(Pass the balloon from one hand to the other.)

Let's run down the field as fast as we can, Chase the balloon, it's part of the plan!

(Run in place, pretending to chase the balloon as it floats away.)

Now, here comes the balloon in the air, Let's jump and catch it, like we don't have a care!

(Jump up high to catch the balloon as it floats down.)

Let's balance on one hand—hold steady, don't fall, Stay like a monster, standing tall!

(Balance on one hand, arms out wide for support.)

Cool Down

After every burst of activity, it's important to slow down and give the body and mind time to rest. Cooling down helps children develop self-awareness, manage their energy levels, and build positive habits around calm and focus.

Breathing for Calm Encourage children to sit or lie comfortably. Take a slow breath in through the nose for three seconds. Hold the breath for a brief moment. Slowly breathe out through the mouth for four seconds, as if blowing a gentle bubble. Repeat three times, noticing how the body feels softer and quieter each time.

Stretch and Relax Invite children to stretch their arms up high, then gently reach down to touch the floor or their toes. Slowly roll shoulders, relax fingers, and let their whole body feel heavy and calm. Mindful Reflection

Ask a few simple questions: What movement made you feel strong today? What made you smile? How does your body feel now that it's resting?

The Science of Stillness Moments of rest help the brain process what has been learned and prepare for new challenges. Mindful breathing and gentle stretching support emotional regulation, focus, and resilience — vital skills for lifelong wellbeing. These quiet endings are as important as the movement itself. They remind every child that they can be active in body, calm in mind, and kind in heart.

Chi Education – The Mindfulness Adventures

Calming, reflective stories that nurture focus, gratitude and emotional awareness. Let's Look Through the Window – Set in an enchanting garden through the changing seasons, this story invites children to pause, observe, breathe and engage with nature's rhythms. The interactive elements and mindful prompts make it ideal for quiet time, bedtime or reflective moments.

Let's Meet Dai the Dragon – This story transports young readers into Welsh landscapes alongside Dai the Dragon, where friend ship, calm breathing and self-belief are woven into the narrative. A perfect blend of imagination and emotional regulation.

Let's Explore the Ocean – A nature-based mindfulness story that encourages children to dive into their imagination, connect with marine settings, and cultivate calm, curiosity and reflective thinking.

Together these stories serve as a companion series to the CHAM movement-books, offering quiet, restorative moments of calm and focus. For more information and to explore the full series, visit: www.chieducation.co.uk/mindfulnessadventures

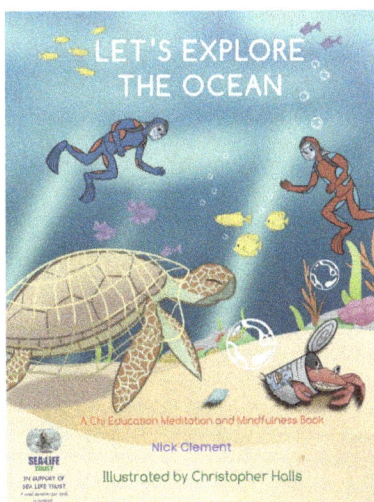

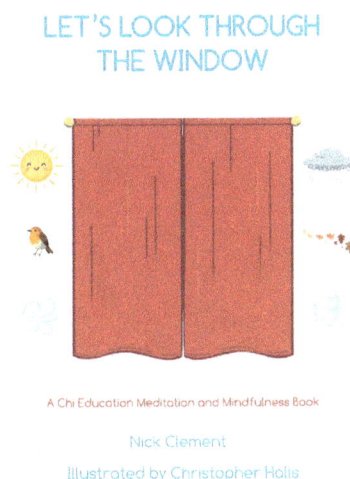

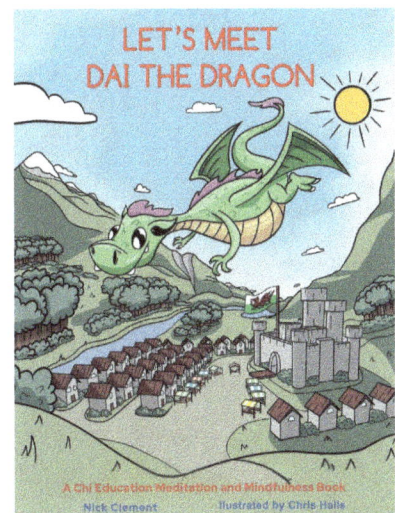

LET'S EXPLORE THE OCEAN
A Chi Education Meditation and Mindfulness Book
Nick Clement
Illustrated by Christopher Halls

LET'S LOOK THROUGH THE WINDOW
A Chi Education Meditation and Mindfulness Book
Nick Clement
Illustrated by Christopher Halls

LET'S MEET DAI THE DRAGON
A Chi Education Meditation and Mindfulness Book
Nick Clement
Illustrated by Chris Halls